POETRY NOW EASTERN 1998

Edited by

Andrew Head

First published in Great Britain in 1997 by
POETRY NOW
1-2 Wainman Road, Woodston,
Peterborough, PE2 7BU
Telephone (01733) 230746
Fax (01733) 230751

HB ISBN 1 86188 732 9
SB ISBN 1 86188 737 X

FOREWORD

Although we are a nation of poetry writers we are accused of not reading poetry and not buying poetry books: after many years of listening to the incessant gripes of poetry publishers, I can only assume that the books they publish, in general, are books that most people do not want to read.

Poetry should not be obscure, introverted, and as cryptic as a crossword puzzle: it is the poet's duty to reach out and embrace the world.

The world owes the poet nothing and we should not be expected to dig and delve into a rambling discourse searching for some inner meaning.

The reason we write poetry (and almost all of us do) is because we want to communicate: an ideal; an idea; or a specific feeling. Poetry is as essential in communication, as a letter; a radio; a telephone, and the main criteria for selecting the poems in this anthology is very simple: they communicate.

Poetry Now Eastern 1998 represents a new set of voices; a flourishing generation of poets in a new landmark in anthologies of modern poetry.

The poems inside have been selected because they communicate directly to the reader. The poets have been inspired by many modern-day issues yet many have simply been inspired by life. The intricacies of human life constantly fascinate us; poetry provides an opportunity to unravel our own personalities and view things from different perspectives.

This collection is varied and innovative but it will grab the reader's interest from the first page to the last.

CONTENTS

THE AWAKENING

The frosts and snows of winter are past
There are early signs of springtime at last,
The leaves on the trees begin to unfold,
And daffodil buds are turning rich gold.
A cluster of snowdrops fringed with green
Nestling 'neath evergreen shrubs can be seen,
The hedgehog awakes from it along winter sleep,
Lambs frisk along by contented sheep.
A proud duck with ducklings waddling behind
Is searching to see if a pond she can find.
In spite of winter's snow, frost and rain,
Everything is coming to life again.
But it is not till we hear the blackbirds sing
That we can herald the coming of spring.

V R Jeffery

Life Upside Down

The middle of June,
Exams are over,
I should be shouting with glee and joy,
Instead I'm upside down in sorrow.
I'm being shouted and screamed at,
For petty little things,
Being abused puts it to an end.
Day in, day out, I hate it so,
I only need help and then I will go.
I cry myself to sleep every night,
Because I'm somebody no-one wants.
I cannot be the person people want,
The person they all call my sister.

I am who I am,
I'll be who I'll be.
With or without I will succeed,
I'll live off the faith in my soul,
I will reach my targeted goal.
The person in me I will seek,
Because every person is unique.

Stephanie Sharp

THE VISITOR

Journey's end is just the beginning; people to visit,
lives to touch -
worlds to cross and laughter to bring.
Mysteries to create by the magic of the soul
travelling on unseen rainbows
into other people's lives.

Electric atmosphere; lights that dazzle - dim - then dazzle again
TVs that click and channels that change
inexplicably . . .
A golden butterfly is lifted from the Christmas tree;
fluttering against the windowpane, miraculously alive,
a bright coloured friend appears;
a symbol of hope.
The snow fall silently.

I am the soul that is the click; the flutter; the light that shines.
I am invisible, but I am here -
a phoenix risen from the ashes of yesterday
to bring joy tomorrow.
I know this house well; it knows me.
The cat's eyes are my eyes; her mistress understands.
The cat stretches; contentment is hers -
and mine.

I am spirit, travelling between two worlds;
an unseen being of light,
crossing the 'Bridge of Life' for an instant today, tomorrow
and for eternity. A reminder of times that weren't quite as lonely . . .
I wish only to share my happiness with those I loved -
and who loved me.
I am no strange force to be feared.
Light is love; love is light.
Love is eternal.
I am love.

Annette Borrill

SOUL OF THE ALBATROSS

Large tears are swept aside
by the bitter wind, as the wide
wings of the albatross send
it skimming over the great
mountains and troughs of the restless ocean.

Forever searching for its soul,
snatched away when it was young
by the sharp edge of a mighty
storm. It now spends its time
winging through the valleys
of endless green seas.

It weep endless tears, desperate
to be united once again. Then
leave the lonely seas forever.
To live on a friendly shore
and always have a place to shelter
when the great storms blow.

Edwin W Branagan

Speak To Me

On this old airfield I stand and stare,
Wondering, what long ago happened there,
You have a presence of sadness and sorrow,
Knowing your time may come tomorrow,
Now derelict and discarded needed no more,
As I close my eyes, I feel your peace not war.

I know that you want to tell me so much,
I feel your vibrations in all that I touch,
Once so majestic in all your glory,
Speak to me, open up, tell me your story
Take me on my journey into your past
I see you, I feel you, I hear you at last.

'Long time ago, when men went to fight,
From the air they found a new kind of might,
Blast bombs, incendiaries, aircraft and machines,
So they built this airfield to serve their means,
I grew from ground ploughed and sown with care,
Crops had grown here from year to year.

Cracked concrete, desecration and buildings that fall,
Once a top secret blueprint on a desk at Whitehall,
My scars deepen as I'm trapped here in time,
Left to serve the sentence of my own war crime,
Each day I wake to the song of the bird,
At night I sleep, only my ghosts can be heard.

Look at my yards, no more lorries to repair,
The old butt wall, no more firing to hear,
My headquarters long gone, forgotten, lost,
Hangars sold years ago, to set off the cost,
My aircraft flew away, never to return,
It's the life and men for which I yearn.

My runways were broken and taken away,
Peri-tracks forgotten, dispersals in decay,
Nissans and Romneys have fallen apart,
Who remembers FIDO to clear fog in the dark,
My bomb dump is lost, in woods overgrown,
A crumbling watch tower stands all alone.

Now in twilight years, I'm tired and alone,
In prime to hundreds I was their home,
One by one they left, where they had trod,
Some found partners, others found God,
I'm so weary now, come back another day,
Remember, it's only for my execution I stay.'

Thank you old airfield, return to your dreams,
Those of hard fought effort, men and machines,
I wish I'd met you in those faraway dark years,
My thoughts join you, and I share your tears,
I will not forget you, I will come again,
Now, go back to sleep and rest forever, Amen.

Susan Priestley

To Stimulate Thought Reflections:

How clear is the glass
How subtle its depth?
How many its facets
How deep and what breadth?

How murky the glass
How clear is its past?
Is it grubby with age
or faulty in caste?

How obscure is the glass
Is its purpose to hide?
Does it shroud inner beauty
or conceal warped inside?

How broken the glass
by what forcible strain?
Was it tempered and shattered
Will it laminate again?

How stained is the glass
with its figures so fine?
Is the pigment vermilion
or the blood of all time?

How false is the glass
How true is its shine?
Is it diamond or ruby
or blown with red wine?

How beautiful the glass
Does it revel in light?
Is its depth a despair
or concealing some might?

How perfect the glass
is it optically sound?
Does it reflect true each surface
the universe round?

How long is the glass
Will it last thro' all time?
Or will the sand run out
At the base of my rhyme?

How clear our conceptions
Each statement refined?
How clear is this world
in each single mind?

Charlie Oades

WAR CRY

So innocent the children
Some tired and weak,
Warm thoughts of home and love they can seek,
War is the terror, they're subjected to find,
Wounds to their bodies, and some of their minds,
Politicians, some argue they're war makers there,
Decisions they make, no risk them bare,
Fight for the country, soldiers forward they step,
Dirty work for politicians and down trodden they're kept,
No mothers or fathers the orphans look on,
Hiding in rubble 'till the bombs have gone,
Little lives could have meaning, just given a chance
But they know hardship and sorrow, love's only a glance.
Sail away on a dream little baby don't cry
One day will come, when it's their turn to die
Live for your dreams, and hope that tomorrow
Peace lives in your hearts and conquers all sorrows.

Karen Webb-Jones

Last Greetings

Do not cry near my grave . . .
When I'll be near you . . .
also feeling a soft breeze shave?
On your tearsome face that will be me too!

Do not cry now? It's too late you see?
Showing feelings in your grief?
While in life showed me such hate . . .
I've forgiven you dear! You must believe . . .

Somehow, I haven't died, spiritually you see
If ever you don't see me standing near . . .
I'm very happy now, I'm bodily free . . .
of your hurting words which broke my heart dear . . .

can never hurt me anymore now!
Your sorrow now! Seeing you in tears!
I'll forgive you, still love you somehow . . .
Take care! I'll be always so near.

Irena Parker

Life Is Not Always What We Plan

I've never been ambitious - a pity you may say
I longed to be just ordinary, and go my own sweet way
There's lots that I would like to do, but I don't long for fame
I really just want to be happy - with everyone else the same
This cannot be - I have found out - for life is not cut and dried
With one set pattern to follow, that has been both tested and tried
It takes all sorts to make the whole, into something really worthwhile
That's why we're all different, with varied views and style
No-one can go their own sweet way - there are others needing care
No-one can live just for themselves, we have to learn to share
We cannot always be happy, for things come to make us sad
We come up against the unpleasant - the ugly and the bad
This is life and we can't expect for everything to go just right
But, we can be sure of one thing - we are always in God's sight
So let us look to Him and find, the strength to carry on
For He in love meets every need - a power to lean upon
So no matter what may happen - or what life brings about
We have a loving saviour - and so many blessings to count
One who is with us throughout each day, a friend who's only
a prayer away.

Fran Merrett

TEENAGE FRIENDS

Of friends we were the very best
Full of laughter, fun and zest
Every moment we would spend together
Never mind the state of the weather
You had a younger brother
To him you were like a mother
Wherever we went he came along
You and I shared the same and favourite song
Playing games, skipping, tiggy and hopscotch
Too busy and happy to ever look at our watch
Fishing with our little nets, going on picnics
Always dressed like hippie beatniks
We never fell out you and I
Never a cross word, never a lie
You like my parents, I only liked your dad
Your mum was never in, when she was always mad
I was lucky, I got lots of love
You did off your dad, all your mum did was give orders and shove
But you didn't care you had me and your brother
Always maintaining you hated your mother
She never appreciated a thing you did
You were a burden, a bloody kid
Life was cruel, we should have grown up together
Our friendship was bonded 'Forever Friends'
You died at 17, my whole world fell apart
Now at 44 years you are still deep in my heart
'What becomes of the broken hearted
Who have loved and now departed'
As short as your life was, I'm glad it started
You were my best mate

Save me a place Deliah, we'll meet again yet
When I hear that song whether it's five or eleven
I know I'll see you again up in heaven
I'll also see your brother Slater
You called for him to join you just two weeks later
Your mum shed tears and did nothing but sit
Never knowing what she had, until she lost it
    Oh well you two
  Rest in peace, I still love you.

E A Brocklesby

Can You Explain?

(Eulogy to those born blind)

I long for the pleasure to feast my eyes
on drifting clouds in summer skies.
I yearn for a glimpse of the setting sun
signalling to all that day is done.
To all but a few these common sights
are no rarer than bright moonlit nights,
and can you explain the harvest moon?
So grand it makes young lovers spoon.
What is silver, what is light?
How do you mean the stars shine bright?
I've tried to imagine all kinds of things,
like buttercups and fairy rings.
Of birds on wing in a gathering storm,
the twilight pause before the dawn.
And lush green meadows with trees so tall,
the morning mist in the autumn fall.
These wondrous things I've never seen.
Can you explain the shades of green?

Keith Hutchins

SON

From the moment I held you
Your tiny little form
My love for you grew, so deep
A perfect gift, to treasure and protect
And as you've grown from baby to toddler
Exploring the world about you, then to school
Learning, making friends, more independent
I've stood back, watching carefully, feeling proud
Being alongside you, learning about you
And the special bond between a mother and a son
And now, nearly a man
I admire you and feel so very proud
To have been able to share life with you
And be a part of a very special person
Who's brought so much purpose
Into people's lives
And when it's your turn
To be blessed with a child
You'll understand the joy and happiness
That a child brings
Thank you son for being you
And giving so much joy.

Thanks Mum.

Adrienne Aspinall

A Warrior's Dream

A bleak and misty dawn rose through rain-washed skies
Black clouds billowed blown by a chill north wind
A man rode a dripping white horse across the moor
His grey cloak wrapped tightly about him.
He drooped in the saddle for in his left shoulder
An arrow was buried deep in his flesh
Death stalked him through the wet heather
He was chilled to the bone
But the fire in his eyes still burned brightly

He needed fire, food and a woman's
Tender loving care to heal him
The man swayed and dropped over onto the horse's neck
Unconscious now and dreaming of home and his woman.
His horse knew the way, and picking up the man's thoughts
bore him home.

John Fraser Feary

Let's Call It Justice

To judges and barristers, heroes of the courts
We'll say for justice you strived,
We'll give you a medal, knight you a sir
On your gravestone we'll say how you thrived.

No innocent man should ever serve time
But no guilty should ever go free,
You decide on a verdict, sentence you pass
But did your eyes, ever really see?

Rape a young child, the worst crime of all
But we'll try to prove that you're sick,
We'll drag up your past, and say you're deprived
That may just do the trick.

Murder mankind, it's twenty five years
But we'll try to prove you're insane,
We'll lock you up, but we'll treat you well
You'll soon be free to kill again.

Start your own massacre, take innocent lives
But we'll try to prove that you're ill,
Let's drag up politics, nations can't rest
Let's call it a war, a licence to kill.

But when your path changes, and you do become
A victim who fell ill to crime,
We'll stand back and listen, watch and do nothing
And know that your soul has served time.

So before you destroy innocent souls,
And become the lowest of lows,
Remember my friend, the truth of the world
Man shall reap what he sows.

Susan Evelyn Churton

The Earth Poem

The world that we live in is in despair,
For the people who live in it simply don't care,
They say they own the earth and cannot be beaten
When they already have by the animals they've eaten

There isn't a solution
To stop pollution
Or hunting for the sheer delight,
They never think of their victim's fright.

Fancy being killed and mounted on a wall,
Or made into a handbag or sold on a stall,
Imagine being hunted day and night,
For your tusks or fur, no matter what your might

When your killer is in view
There is nothing you can do,
Yet God only set humans to live on the earth,
To guard and protect every creature
From the day of its birth.

What's now was never meant to be,
But what's the use?
You won't listen to me.

Nicola Gooch (10)

ONLY YESTERDAY

Was it only yesterday, I held your hand to cross the street
Was it just last night you came to me,
Wanting just a cuddle in the middle of the night
Throwing arms around me, lovingly.

Was it only yesterday I bought you that new dress,
The pink one, trimmed with bows of lilac lace.
You wore it on that special day and, oh! You looked so sweet,
The colours seemed to suit your pretty face.

Was it only yesterday you went out on your own,
You went to visit friends you'd met at school,
I trembled as I watched you go, my heart was in my mouth,
You must have thought that I was just a fool.

Was it really yesterday you were my little girl,
The one who used to climb upon my knee.
Now you seem so tall and strong and carefree as the wind
But it seems like only yesterday to me.

Joan Burrows

Heat Wave

Suffering in silence
summer's sweltered heat
blistered toes
tired, aching feet
itching, scratching
coat of biting flies
false hope
unfettered wind softly sighs
stirring dust-coated leaves
from their sun-baked path
disturbing groggy wasps
buzzing their wrath
moisture flows
sweat soaked pores
toiling in the heat
completing chores
soaking up the sun
inflamed with burning pain
lips cracked and sore
whisper prayers for cooling rain

Luke Thomas

Untitled

Reflections on a rainy night
Clip clack clip clack of high heeled shoes
Hurry past the windows not wanting to choose
Others just dawdle collars turned up high
As they gaze into the shops and then just sigh
They walk onto the pavements which are shiny and wet
Their mackintoshes glisten as they get very wet
Umbrellas drip and puddles splash about
As children wearing wellingtons jump in and out
As the light pours from the windows onto the wet ground
The reflections and the colours are turned upside down
As the rain is still pouring from the clouds up above
People hurry home for tea to the home that they love

Jean Miller

The Wreck

Rusting hulk
nestled in overgrown grass
dirty seats covered
shattered windscreen glass
pocked red paint
peeling, flaking
wheels of motion
long past braking
engine parts pillaged
scavengers, the human kind
carcass ripped, torn
whatever they find
innards coated black, sticky
leaking oils
metal shell, littered
broken spring, coils
wires exposed, dashboard smashed
scattered fuses, fractured bulbs
soiled seats slashed
hinges wrenched, doors hanging
grubby sponge overflowing
man's loyal servant, abandoned
buried in funeral weeds growing

Paul Birkitt

SHIPYARD

Once a great shipyard stood beside fast flowing Trent
filling many acres of open ground, opposite the town
Footpath open to the public ran across its ground
leading to villages, via riverbanks of muddy brown
Lying in their hundreds undisturbed for many years
stout trunks of oak trees, stripped of wrinkled bark
Covered over by nettles creeping and thistles seeding
half-buried in a tumble of weeds where children lark
Sawyers busied themselves, cutting and chopping wood
attending massive skeletal frames standing on the stocks
Planking over naked ribs, ships starting to take shape
piles of timber looming tall on Gainsborough docks
Extending across one side of the yard a rope-walk
stretching over open fields, constructed of wood and tile
Inside men busied themselves with bundles of hemp
amidst the turning wheels, shouting voices, rank and file
Largest employer of the time on Gainsborough town
building and launching ships here for centuries past
Remnants of buildings, ruinous shells littler the site
old saw-pits overgrown with thorn and bramble fast
Everywhere you look abandoned wrecks, a graveyard
of things ruined and rendered useless by age
The ground all about hidden beneath a spongy blanket
scattered wood-chips and sawdust, a thickly growing stage
Surrounding air filled with lingering fumes of boiling tar
black smoke billows from the tar boiler's crumbling shack
Age old trunks sinking in the ground over passing time
delivered years before, left to weather dirty black
Purchased by shipwrights for the building of dreams
fashioned and seasoned in time-honoured ways
Gainsborough shipyard on the banks of the River Trent
established here way back in Elizabethan days

Chris Birkitt

Bosnia Blighted

The sound of the child crying haunts me.
So far away is this little one in her desolate misery.
Hundreds of miles separate us, as does the vast yawning chasm
of the ever-changing sea.
I view her plight on the evening news.
It's dark outside, yet no darkness could ever compare
to that of her memories blackened and soiled by the bitterness
which has marred her land, torn it apart at the very seams,
broken her heart.
She looks so small against the rugged backdrop of the hills
where snipers hide waiting to cut down another youthful stem.
Her delicacy only serves to emphasise her pain.
Thin, undernourished cheeks, huge, frightened eyes.
Her hands reach out in a pleading gesture, then fall limply
at her side, exhaustion overcoming that weary body.
Enemy soldiers stand expressionless.
Have they forgotten what it is to feel?
She hasn't.
Her mother died yesterday in the fire which is bluntly termed
'Ethnic Cleansing'.
I cannot believe how cruel they can be, how disgustingly evil
as to consider clean the day they murdered a loving mother
and took the light of innocent happiness out of a child's eyes.

Marie Leonie Cheetham

Sober Reflections

Social and economical sciences lag far behind
The technological progress of mankind
Leaving us in limbo 'tween an out-moded past
And a frightening future coming on too fast
Firm moral values or religious belief
Formerly gave individuals mental relief
Now horizons undreamed of in past days
Open myriad opportunities in unknown ways

Ernie Kay

One True Religion

Throughout centuries man has founded many religions,
Many of whom had condemned different consecrations,
Through hate and prejudice that led to assassinations.
'Judge not that you be judged,' Jesus taught, 'love thy assailant.'
Why were those lines not heeded by many generations?
Two thousand years on sustained are wars and persecution.
Which religion today would Jesus praise for perfection?
Perhaps all. Perhaps a few. Or perhaps none yet known.
Jesus would welcome those that give absolute loving,
Harmony to foreigners and peace amongst everyone,
Respect for beliefs of different cultures and nations.
'Ye shall know ye by thy fruits,' Jesus once truly mentioned.
True creeds. whatever their rituals, find something matching,
Practising and preaching to love and to harmonise,
With all the world regardless of status, culture or nations.
There can be only one true universal religion,
Natural common sense laws like universal motions.

Louis Don Barrow

A Pup

My mistress tries to teach me but I'm a scatter brain you see,
But I can tell the difference 'twix a lamppost and a tree.
I'm often getting scolded for things I should not do,
Like scratching up the carpet or chewing up a shoe;
But when I look appealing she always does relent,
Oh I can judge her feelings, she thinks that I repent.

I chase a ball to please her, she really thinks it's fun
And boasts to all her friends how really fast I run
I love to run through puddles then through the open kitchen door,
Then look at my paw marks on the spotless kitchen floor.
My mistress she will scold me, but when I hang my head in shame,
She picks me up and cuddles me and says it's all a game.

She taught me how to beg and offer up a paw,
She says that I am perfect and can never spot a flaw.
I do not like my vet, he sticks needles in my scruff,
So I bit his little finger just to show him that I'm tough.
It's great to be a puppy - a darling little tyke,
But it may alter when I'm older, then I'll tell you what it is like.

A Noble

THE SEEKER

Leave me be, leave me be! Leave me in my reverie!
Slumber on, slumber deep! Let me have my hurt to keep!

Aaah! The pain, the pain! The endless sand,
my head, my head, it's coming free.
Discreet I said, not with a hammer
you've brought me back to all this clamour.

A soldier of fortune, I'll seek again,
with formless lips and memories.
Of that which you were and what you'll become,
in the wherever you are.

Ah! The iniquitous battle!
Ethereal glimpses without the seeing.
Tantalising caresses without the touching.
Without the touch, I'd not have looked.
Without the look, I'd not have touched.

Assuage my discontent, lay down your arms,
for once; relent!

C Wuin

An Aged Hippie

He owes it to a sixties kind of scene,
All his faded pop memorabilia:
The signed photographs, the singles and the albums,
The T-shirts and the statuettes, the drum kit,
The guitars and the floral ties, his taste
In music and in women, all the love
That he has ever made, and the much greater
Love he has not made; he owes it all
To a sixties kind of scene, to *doing one's own thing*,
Much as he has done for the last thirty years
And as I have done
                    for the last eleven lines.

Stan Downing

A True Friend

Bumping into this and that
Alas! My independence fading fast.

That cherry bough I know
Has gone white with spring.

The lark I hear up there
Upon the wing.

To see my Grandson
When he smiles and tells me
Of a sunset in the sky.

The snow I feel, but cannot see
Its brilliance looking back at me.

No longer may I stroll
Along the paths I knew so well.

Alas! Again despair sets in -

And then . . . and then . . .

A precious gift I did receive,
A lick was felt upon my face
A paw upon my knee -

My life had returned
As *Ben* my guide-dog
Would see for me.

Irene Isabell Brown

Rear View

Big bums, small bums,
Wobbling everywhere,
This is the view I get, from my wheelchair.
Children are as tall as I
As they quickly run on by.
People look, well, people stare,
When they see me in my chair.
It isn't red, or a bright fluorescent pink!
It doesn't emit a nasty stink!
Why do they stare, and look so glum.
It's just an ordinary looking one.
They look more miserable.
Than I ever could become.
Big bums, small bums,
Wobbling everywhere.
Why should I worry.
Why should I care.
(With sight such as these,)
Who wants to stand and stare!
The view's much funnier
From my wheelchair.
May as well sit, and enjoy the view.
Thinking after all,
I'm no funnier looking
Than you!

Constance Roper

OPEN YOUR EYES WIDE!

Art is in the eye of the beholder,
Maybe it's in a museum,
Or even in your kitchen.
It can be in a painting,
Done by a really great master.
But the best, is the special one,
Brought home from school.
Do you really look like that?
Orange hair on end and matchstick legs.
But in your eyes its worth
Is every bit of money that you have.
Of course, a work of art
Is a well cooked meal
And a table nicely set with silver shining,
Look at a rainbow, in all those colours
Did God upset the paintbox?
A poem written from the heart
Is read maybe by many.
A pleasure brought to aching hearts.
Have you watched a dragonfly flitting about?
All those lovely colours.
Have you got a garden set with flowers?
It's someone with an artistic eye,
To get all the colours to mingle nicely.
If we see something lovely
It gives your aching heart a warm glow.
This all makes life worth living,
From now on, all of you keep your eyes wide open!

Margaret Pearce

Nature And Man

Man is trivial and small
when nature calls upon its force
to overthrow its usual course
and return to the chaos - its source

Man is trivial and weak
when he attempts to seek
his interpretation
to the roots of creation

Man is trivial but blessed
with a mind obsessed
to explore
nature's source and its course.

Wila Yagel

God's Studio

Of all life's imagery and imagination of great artists captured on canvas, faith has remained elusive from the artist's brush.

For only the canvas of our mind, can create the artwork of faith, from the palette of belief in our heart.

Valerie Taber

Confession

Innocent youth. How long ago it seems,
  When half of my time was spent in my dreams.
The waiting, the longing, to see *that* dear face.
  How coincidental to be at the same place!
The fancies, the doubts, the passion, and fears,
  The heartbreak of quarrels which ended in tears.
How could my heart heal after bearing such pain?
  But, oh! . . . The next time when I loved once again!
So many times did I love in the past,
  Until I met you, my true love, at last.

Kathleen Abbott

ALONE

I am locked out all
alone. The clouds are
grayer. They move
faster into night.

The cold wind
blows across my face
and my hair won't
stay in one
place.

Crunched up in
a corner I sit here
wondering when she'll
come home.

It's getting darker
and I am still all alone.
The street lights have
already come on.

It's getting darker
and colder but I am
still all alone.

Mindy LaRouche

PLAN 17

Sun
Shining
Down
Trees growing up
Man cutting down

Sun
Shining
Down
Children growing up
Man cutting down

Sun
Shining
Down
Nothing Growing up
Man finished

Sun
Son?
What!
Nothing
Nothing

Allen Meade

WOMAN

I am woman, I am strong in the midst of pain
I am woman, when kicked down I rise again
I am woman, you will never see me cry
I am woman, no matter what the job I'll try
I am woman, you beat me but I feel no pain
I am woman, I can bear your child but not your name
I am woman, you rape my body but you
Cannot reach my mind
I am woman, you are cold when you try to
Be kind,
I am woman, I have enough love for all
Mankind
I am woman . . . but you are man, and you
Are blind.

Margery Hadnum

SENSES

A kiss can be for the moment
  or proof of forever
    of hopes and wishes sent
      of sunshine dreams, whatever the weather.

A touch can be a reminder
  Can be a message of, 'I care',
    That special touch could not be kinder
      That gentle stroke through your hair.

The sight of your loved one sleeping
  The rise and fall of life,
    A giggle from a dream happening
      Like a child, so free from strife.

A soft voice can be beguiling
  But with no strength can let you down,
    While the stern can leave you quaking
      No doubt said, with a frown.

But when arrives that moment,
  That sinks you till you're soaked,
    That voice, that lifts your lament,
      That evident, 'togetherness' leaves you choked.

These senses are your building blocks
  With them build your marriage wall,
    Together in life take your knocks
      But sense your strengths and you'll not fall.

K Taylor

THINK OF ME

Think of me when I have gone
Remember that the soul lives on
Don't be sad that I'm not here
Remember I am very near
Carry on in your usual way
Live your life from day to day
Be happy when you think of me
Remember that my spirit's free
For I am ever by your side
I'm there to watch and help and guide
For I know one day you'll be with me
No matter how long those years may be
I'll care for you and watch and wait
Until we meet at the golden gate

Christine Corby

Enter To Inter

As if time was escaping,
But of no consequence to me,
Caught in any brief moment,
Delusions of my ecstasy.
Enchantment of a higher kind,
Falters unwillingly before,
Ghostly echoes of my past,
Harangue my weakened door.
I could, no doubt, in time forget,
Just as my animation ebbs,
Kill off all terrors that persist,
Let loose restraining webs.

Mark Bayliss

TOURISTS

Tourists at last have found us in Fenland
It's taken some time, they usually want sand
But they seem to be straying this way at last
And we must make them realise we don't live in the past

There's lots to enjoy, fishing, boating and birds
There's Cathedrals, museums and creatures in herds
The Tourist Board, will offer help and advice
The folk in the office are always quite nice

So let us have time for the tourists each day
If they ask for help when they lose their way
It costs us nothing to smile or offer advice
So be kind, keep them coming, it's nice to be nice

Kim Fountain-Hoare

Death

To me, happiness has no meaning
No apparent definition,
I cry, I starve, I hurt, I die.
When I need a big strong hug,
To reassure me from this helpless life,
All I get is a bag of bones and a cup of rice,
Why is it me, who starves and cries,
When you're all leading greedy hateful lives,
What did I do?
What crime did I commit?
Is being me such an evil sin?
You just look at me on TV,
Alone in pain, helpless on the floor,
What is my purpose please
To live as an exhibition?
God let me die,
I can't take it anymore,
But that's too merciful,
I have to put up with watching my family
And friends die,
And all for what?
A bloody stupid war.

Elisabeth Crouch

I Know Him

Racing thumping pounding heart
If only he would come back
We could make a fresh start
What of our home the children we have raised
Our years together sure something's to be saved

I know every inch each line on his face
Only I should feel his loving embrace
I know his habits both good and bad
I know what makes him happy, sad and mad

Yes, you're the victor at this time it's clear
I'll fight for him. Yes I will, my dear
I don't think you're ugly, I'm sure you're quite nice
You want my man? You'll pay the price

We've been together for years and years
He's made me happy, he's had me in tears
We were in union, united and strong
Can't you see what you're doing is wrong

Wake up sugar, stop acting so dim
You're forgetting one thing
I know him.

Tracy Bellamy

Other World

Deep below the ground where daylight never comes,
Beneath the roots of mountains never warmed by the sun.
There are vast and mighty caverns,
Where the strangest folk do dwell,
Mining there for crystals, silver and gems.

Lighting their way with brands soaked in oily tar,
Diamonds in the rocks glimmer like lost and lonely stars.
By secret lakes and cold still pools,
They carve out great halls of stone.
Palaces of grandeur in which they make their home.

In fiery volcanic furnaces they forge their metal wares.
Hammers, picks and anvils; and jewellery ornate and fair.
Gold rings and golden sceptre has their mighty king,
While brooches set with sapphires and emeralds sparkling green,
With delicate silver necklaces adorn his gracious queen.

Their interconnecting tunnels form a tortuous maze,
And strangers wandering into them can be lost for days.
Here one must be wary, always on one's guard.
For glowering in the shadows, spreading fear and dread,
Dragons lie in waiting with eyes of ruby red.

Magnificent and resplendent are these awesome beasts,
Their scales as iridescent as that of amethyst.
Guardians of the treasure vaults.
With their breath of golden flame.
None will they let enter, except those that did them tame.

P K George

ANTIPEMINE

In terror's fields they plant no rice
the crop that's sown so out of line
the harvest hiemal, reapers random
ravaged innocence posts the sign

the ways of war are ever present
the teeth of dogs are seldom drawn
the walking hands, a rough-hewn balance
for fruits no plucked but only shorn

sunrays warm once verdant branches
soft rain kisses missing limbs
memories and good tomorrows
wasted by greed's shrieking winds

countless millions, living corpses
fearful of their date with time
spectres of a present future
with man and men well out of chime.

a village green in high point summer
clatter, chatter dress the morn
the artist's daub, a differing picture
where the stumps are seldom drawn.

love would stir a sleeping conscience
but bottom lines still rule the head
No savage combine blade discarded
until all hope is cropped and bled.

L G Stiles

DUMBING-DOWN

He wasn't thick, you know? He just
didn't get the help he needed.
One soul lost amongst fifteen hundred-odd,
Came in behind the rest. Left behind the rest. No change there.
It's the battery system, a source
of great discomfort to me for years.
Instead of getting him to do anything useful, they
get him to paint a picture.
'Can't do your two times table? Do a picture,'
He should have been good at sport. They'd have liked that.

And then he left a few weeks before me. By that
time there was little point
in him staying. No pictures left to paint. Probably
not the cash to provide the paintbrushes anyway.

A year on I walk down the street, avoiding
piles of dog muck and a dead seagull
and am laughed at twice
for wearing a hat on the hottest day of the year. I
groan inwardly.
Last thing I heard he was 'working on the machines'.
They've got him now.
Pity, that.

Andrew Brain

For Millie

For Millie who brought me roses;
did she know I loved them so?
That a bouquet of roses is more than that
but a garden I knew long ago.
A terrace of roses, clouds of pink blooms,
banks of pale yellows cooling the stone
and scenting the air on a hot afternoon.

That lovely oasis in suburbia's maze,
the road to school in summer's drowse,
are drawn in the map of childhood days.
I can still smell the perfume that hung on the air,
I can still see the colour that soothed the eye,
so a garden of roses, or a just one bloom
is walking to school on a warm afternoon.

Elizabeth Beck

RIVERSIDE SPRING AT ELY

The riverside with lacy tracery is hung,
Swift flowing currents chilled by winter's breath
Carry stately sails of swans along,
And drakes preen courting feathers in the warming sun.

Shrouded craft roll back their winter keep;
Hooded eyelet ports blink in the new bright light;
Yawning cabin doors inviting friends aboard
To launch the spring, shake bearths from chilly sleep.

Reads rustle drily last year's woody spears
Protecting promise of new life and birth;
Fenland water meadows ankle deep and still
Diamond glinting shafts of warmth appears.

The dormant peace of winter now gives way
To family outings and the ice-cream van;
Brave lightclad couples wander slowly on
Dream of bedroom suites and the wedding day.

The Cutter Inn spills out its noisy smell
Of hops; folk celebrating winter's passed;
Coats shed dark lensed animinity put on,
To taste the sun and feel that all is well.

And overall the Great Ships there
Brooding shadows of paternal love,
Witness to winters past and spring again,
With God's great goodness for all to share.

Joy Perry

THE PATRIACH OF THE NEW ENGLISH

Born in the year of our Lord 1264,
He nurtured our language from the spoken core,
French and Latin were the written word of their courts,
To have written English was in Manning's thoughts.

Studying in Cambridge at St Edwards Hall,
And to Sempringham Priory was Manning's call,
Defined by the sounds of the South Lincolnshire Hills,
Stories were told through Manning's precious quills.

It was to the Gilbertine Priory at Sixhills
Manning sharpened the English literary skills,
Paving the way for Edward Spencer and Shakespeare,
Here's to a proud English literature career.

His job to translate in rhyme of moral tales,
In the streets of Bourne his name prevails.
At the time of his death was born a great pioneer
Called Chaucer to a fine literary career.

Marcus Tyler

Philosophical About Builders

Them geezers said the job's too hard
To get all done in just one day
'Ain't got the tools 'ere in our bag,
Sorry mate,' I heard them say.
But still they stayed
And still they played
That blasted radio all day.
And whistled to the mindless tunes,
And used a rule
Instead of spoons
To stir their tea
At 10 and 3,
And then they went home at 4
Leaving shavings on the floor
And did not even stop to say -
Oh well, they'll start again next day!

Peter Dean

Small Things

Control your wish to do great deeds.
Do not forget the little needs:
The kindly act, the helping hand.
Try earnestly to understand
And to consider others more,
Than you may have done before.
We aim in life at grandiose schemes,
Then often find they are but dreams.
While focused on that distant goal,
We fail to see the needy soul
Close by, who may need just a smile
To make them feel that life's worthwhile.
Happiness lies in little deeds
Performed to meet each other's needs.

Patrick Murphy

For Catherine (Wherever She May Be)

Let us, in this full silence of the night,
sit face to face and with no sound uttered
but the soft rhythm of our breathing,
speak, as lovers, each secret word one to the other.

Let our eyes linger for longer moments than we can count,
as our lips meet and in silence pour forth such
words of passion, as would cause the very stars
to linger for yet longer moments to listen.

And in those moments my arms shall be a fortress
about you and my love shall be as a vast army
to protect you and my hands shall be as bright
armour upon you and my heart shall put upon you
such wings that you will soar above all enemies.

John A Williams

THE MOON

When I was just a little girl, the moon was made of cheese,
I watched it from my bed at night, peeping through the trees
It raced behind the big dark clouds a wondrous golden ball
I'd close my eyes for just awhile and it wasn't there at all.

When I had grown a few more years the moon took on a face,
I learned at school just what it was and why it changed its place.
It seemed quite unbelievable it was so far away,
Why did it only shine at night in that ghost-like kind of way.
It disappears in daylight, but then the stars do too.
And was it laughing, 'Ha, ha, ha,' or was it saying 'O, oo.'

Then came the day that men went up in rockets to the sky
To find out just what made it shine and where and how and why,
They brought back dust and bags of rock, for boffins here below,
I wonder if they'll ever find just what they want to know.
But there's another reason why the moon's up there above
It's up there for the people who hold hands and fall in love.

Marie Rose Elliott

For You

A seedling in my mind was sown
A flower in my mind has grown
And love's voice sang the loudest at that time

A cool wind blowing in my face
But love has found a warmer place
Inside my heart, a feeling so sublime

A tender touch, a secret thought
A feeling that cannot be bought
Is something sitting softly by my side

And though the miles have come between
We're held by something quite unseen
Its name is love; its strength we cannot hide

Like blossom on a springtime tree
It stands out proud and says to me
You see this thing, its strength is shining through

And now I know we'll never part
These words are spoken from my heart
And every single one is meant for you

Andy Hutchcraft

THE LINKS

Outside, white tundra,
Indoors, a scarlet scullery.
Expectant mongrel, angled head.
We plough the heath and scatter
A smothering of powdered crystal.
A livid yellow sky with floating crows
And jagged crippled trees.
The Redwings raid remaining haws.
Then back to vitriolic flames
And a warming Tetley brew
Our hands held to the pyre.
While large Dark enshrouds a flickering room.
Those heavy drapes exclude the Whirling Dervish.
Within the bounds of patchy rug we're safe,
And crackling fir cones, scent effuse
To blend with steak and kidney
Crispy crust and Bay Leaf tinge.
Lemon rings rotate on steaming wine.
We two simply sit,
Nothing's said:
There is no need.

Roger Osborn

WORDS OF LOVE

Worry not my darling
the day will soon be here
When we can be together
And be happy through the years.

No truer words I've spoken
when I say my love is true
The sun it shines upon your face
And takes away the blues.

The thing I love about you most
it is beyond compare
No matter what I say or do
You always seem to care

I wish I could put into words
the things I want to say
My love for you it seems to me
Just grows from day to day.

Pat Brushett

WILL YOU COME TO ME MY LOVE

Will you come to me my love
When my heart beats so loud
You can no longer bear to hear it?
Or when my cries, so wretched,
Simply tear at your resolve?
Will you come to me my love
When my fingers have bled
From the constant clawing at your vacillation?
Or when my arms have fallen
From the agony of their prolonged, extended pose?
Will you come to me my love
When I whisper so sweetly
That I shall wait forever?
Or when my blanket of scorn
Finally smothers your childlike reason and excuse?

Oh, no my love.
No, I fear you will come
Only after I have fled in dismal disenchantment.

Christine Patient

THAT'S LIFE

My fingers aren't as nimble as they used to be
I cannot thread a needle without much difficulty
It seems the tops of jars are stuck with super glue
and I reckon the eye of the needle has a blob or two

It's time I did away with stairs and had a lift installed!
My hips and knees aren't speaking, and neither can be fooled
It's not the stairs that's creaking as if the boards are loose
It's my old bones a shrieking 'Why don't we call a truce!'

I remember when I was a girl the banister was a slide
A cushion and a piece of rope made it a pony ride
With brother's guns and father's hat a cowgirl I became
then I turned into a vet when my horse was lame

The streets were then a playground no cars to bar our way
I used to ride my bike a lot and play outside all day
We played the Mr Wolf game and buzz against the wall
We'd have to dart around a lot so that we'd miss the ball!

I sit and have a cup of tea with thoughts of days gone by
When I was young and nifty and worked from morn till nigh
I gave no thought how life would be when I was old and grey
Although my mother often said 'You'll be like me one day!'

Janice Tidy

SENSES

Would you move that chair for me,
Please put it near the door,
I've knocked my leg on it, left there,
In the middle of the floor.

Outside a thrush is singing,
I can hear him very clear,
His song becomes more noisy, now
As he sees a cat appear.

The smell of morning dew,
Is very sweet to me,
Honeysuckle is my favourite, and
The strong scent of sweet pea.

It's chilly now, let's go in,
And have a cup of tea,
I think I've left the sugar out,
This doesn't taste right to me.

My senses all work very well,
That is except for one,
My eyes are closed, I cannot see,
Have been blind since life begun.

Pamela Girdlestone

How?

Blood sang a song on his lips
and brains seeped through his teeth
as he struggled to meet truth and
shake its hand!

How to sweep such life under the carpet?
How to close the door so bitterly on an unknown
Sweetness?

How to close your eyes to such beauty
How to stop your heart to such love?

David Hole

My Family

The harbour of love that is my family
Nurtures me and keeps me safe.
Safe from the harsh realities of life.
They shelter me from sadness
And all that is evil.
They support me as a trellis
Supports a tiny climbing plant
And protect me as a suit of armour
Protects a battling knight.
I am content.
Content as a cat basking lazily in the sun.
I am loved.
And yet I take all this for granted.

Charlotte Kime

RUBY

She is daddy's little angel,
And her name describes her as the precious
Little gem stone that she is,
It is hard to comprehend just how precious she is,
Her daddy needs her, she is his heart,
But she is the only remainder from his exploded world,
Her innocence and purity can only cause us to weep inside,
Yet feel humble at the same time,
You see, without knowing,
She has helped her daddy begin to rebuild,
The only satisfaction he can have is their punishment,
'Hatred is a wasted emotion'.
At least he knows Ruby is safe,
But so should her mother,
How can we ever apologise?
Poor, poor Ruby,
She will grow never to know the woman who bore her,
Yet the only possible memory that Ruby will have,
Will be the stillness of her body,
The pitch of her pain,
Or even the brightness of her blood,
The photograph on the mantelpiece can only
Remind them both of the happy little family
That was,
The family that Ruby will never know.

Ceri Stokes

Loss

She brushed his face
With the bird's wing of her hand
Then she sang
Into his shoulder with her sadness.

Andrew Baily

SIGHT

Something that frightens,
Or maybe heightens,
Your happiness in life.
Something you enjoy,
Or maybe to annoy,
And cause trouble and strife.
Something unexpected,
Or maybe you rejected,
And had left behind.
Something going rotten,
Or maybe long forgotten,
Out of sight, out of mind.
We perceive the world through senses,
From behind curtains or fences,
But let us spare a thought
For those who cannot see,
They are just like you and me,
And to help them we ought.

Andrew Fisher

The Wheat Is Not So Yellow Now

Its colour has turned creamy white.
The moon at night is changing, too,
It rolls just like a flame-red ball,
Advising farmers to reap all
They can before the autumn's through.

Seed sown almost a year ago
Thrust up stalks, leaves, and then its ears,
When it could trust spring to remain.
A harvester drones up the lane
In a few busy hours, it clears

Great EU subsidised prairies,
Although grey clouds arrive to smudge
Skies over cereal-grown hills,
Pale with wheat-grist for working mills.
The grain's firm to the driver's touch.

Gillian Fisher

ONLY A DREAM

Life is empty without you.
I know you will never be mine.
It was all over before it started,
but I love you.
I want to take care of you.
I want to cherish you,
but it can never be.
Life brought us together
for a brief instant and took us apart again.
No-one knows why? Only God.
My broken heart is longing for a sign,
longing for tenderness and love
but no-one is listening.
Happiness can never be.

P M Watson

MANOR HOUSE

Captured on film, in nineteenth century prime
a frozen image on the pages of time
Gainsborough Old Hall, with unfurling wings
Manor House visited by England's kings
fruit trees blossom in spring's early bloom
walled garden and orchard, plenty of room
servants stone cottage adjoined to the main
within easy reach of the master's rein
connected via decorative paths and routes
brick north tower, where the wise owl hoots
dominating the corner, rising to the sky
offering a bird's-eye view, way up high
sprawling Gainsborough Town huddles below
creeping ivy steals up the wall, to slowly grow
surrounding the solid wooden door in leaf
unoiled metal hinges groan, creaking with relief
a hundred panes of glass reflecting heat
shed welcome sunlight upon cold floors, warming feet
extending across the mass of the eastern side
bringing illumination to gloomy rooms inside
a plethora of chimneys, columns and stacks
pots of all sizes, lined with a dusting of sooty blacks
sitting upon sloping roofs of tile and slate
billowing smoke, from wood burnt in smouldering grate
tall arched windows set in stone, watch lonely vigil
shadows of the northern face, unfurl beneath shady sill
situated by the riverside, witness to sail and mast
epicentre of Gainsborough Town's historical past.

Chris Bailey

For Someone Special - Devotion

You may not always understand me.
You might question and wonder why
The things I do
The things I say
The reasons why I cry
Don't try to find the logic
Or try to understand the reasons
The answers are deep within my heart
And not within my mind
I did not want very much from life
Simple things some take for granted
Someone to love, to be a mother and wife
So I've been given these precious gifts
And I'm sorry if it seems a little selfish
To keep these treasures to myself
The things I've always wanted.
So when you ask those questions
And want the answers why
Please don't look any further
I've given you my life.
With love.

Sam

Shadow Of The Clouds

As you stand alone in a field,
the shadow of a cloud engulfs you,
a greyness is all that surrounds,
suddenly no noise, no sound,
your feelings are in a timeless void.

You are just hanging there,
suspended in a semi-conscious state.
No way to turn, nowhere to go,
your lifeless body stands below,
a zombie stands, its soul afloat,
up in the air among the clouds,
swirling around like the wind.

As your soul starts to return,
the shadow of yourself darkens, and you are back,
back beneath the floating clouds above.

Roy Bristow

Second Post

No I haven't been swept away with the wind,
Or gone out with the tide,
My correspondence is all behind,
And your letter is here by my side.

I meant to answer right away,
And tell you all my adventures,
But several people came to stay,
Really delightful creatures!

We went here and there
With never a care
Enjoying the thrill of the chase,
Bankruptcy now I must face.

Down to the bone,
Must take out a loan,
Off to Aberdeen for a visit,
Perhaps we'll see Glenlivet.

Maisie Russell-Clements

Calm

Serene, serene, where are you?
Are you in the dreams,
Or the lovers' kiss?
Do you lie in a goal's achievement,
Or in the family breast?
Are you hidden in a job,
Or in the eye of God?
In this modern world,
Do you exist at all?

P Benton

Gossip

Don't just stare and wander away,
Sit there wondering about it for another day,
Stop and think about how it feels,
Spending you days in a chair with wheels.

The painful stare in your eyes,
Standing there gossiping, listening to the lies,
We're not really different, or at all strange,
Not like a new toy from a different range.

We're not a show or a theatre play,
If you are puzzled just stop and say,
We may not be able to run or dance,
But we could be your friend if you gave us the chance.

Frances Ryan (11)

SAD - TO - SEE

Muddled thoughts
In misty minds,
Happy memories
Left behind.
Hospital wards
Full of people,
Old and sick,
Frail and feeble.
All alone
In a strange place,
Glassy eyes,
In expressionless face.
Trapped by age,
A mind defeated,
Weary and worn,
A body depleted.
It's sad to see,
And sorry to say,
This is how the majority,
May end their days.

Polly Cox

KNOWING

What have I done to make you so unkind?
You sad that this passion that fires my soul
Was mutual, but you left me behind.
Your going has made in my world a hole,
That cleaves my heart with never-ending pain.
To see you now casts shadows in my mind
Of all the times that in your arms I've lain;
I prized those moments, but then I was blind
To think I saw adoring in your eyes,
When all I was, was a way to pass time.
So I watch as my heart to the sky flies,
With my emotions tolling their last chime.
The world is stained with a deep shade of blue,
Knowing that I'm sad, knowing I love you.

Yvette Day

GOING HOME

The way is steep
And I am tired
But my Lord is here beside me
To help me along
From day to day
And even carry me part of the way,
But when in time I see the light
Of that beautiful place unknown
I shall rejoice
Because at last I know
That I am going home.

Vera Conolly

JENNA

Jenna is my darling
Jenna is my love
Eyes forever shining
She's gentle as a dove
Her smile is like the sunshine
On a dark and dreary day
She's cheerful and as beautiful
As the sweet spring flowers in May.

J Corr

The Beautiful Lady

The most beautiful clothes on the most beautiful lady,
The best of them all, well maybe.
She has the prettiest dress and the prettiest face,
her hat and her gloves both trimmed with lace.
Her very long hair is so very pretty,
She is not at all the least bit witty.
She's the best of friends with Aunty Meg,
Even though she's just a dolly peg.

Laura Rossington

TIME

Where do you end?
Your vast frontiers push out to the edges of eternity.
What do you know?
Stars lie scattered like broken promises across the bruised evening sky.
Where do you go?
Vanishing like an echo into the distant realms of oblivion.
Somehow,
Somewhere,
Maybe we'll never know.

Sarah Inman

The Scale Of Things

Tadpoles in a jar.
Terrapins trapped in a tank;
Sharks feed in the sea,
What persuades man to capture
And to enshrine these creatures?

We can observe them.
Can protect the rare species,
Ensure they are safe.
Though they move round in circles,
Is that what life is about?

Man, like these creatures,
Is imprisoned on this earth;
Forced into choices,
Making decisions he hates.
Who controls what is to come?

Dawn Shearsmith

SECURE

When we're tired and cold
And it's rained forever more
We enter our homes
And feel warm and secure.

Switch on the kettle
For a warming cuppa
Slip into our slippers
Then sit down to supper.

Turn on the TV
Pull down the blind
Relax get comfy
Feet up and unwind.

Sandman's calling
What utter bliss
A nice warm bed
Home sweet home is this.

Uncertain

When we're cold and tired
And it's rained forever more
We're sheltering in doorways
Or freezing on the floor.

Plastic bags protect our feet
Our heads and body too
We'd love a good hot cuppa
It would warm us thro'.

We'd like to sit and watch TV
To relax and unwind
But until we have a refuge
We're the homeless of mankind.

Sleep comes to everyone of us
God made us all the same
We'd love to be secure and warm
The pavement is a pain.

Chris Baldwinson

SILENT THOUGHTS

No-one came today.
The silent hours were spent in thoughts of you.
My first thought through September's pain,
My love for you those agonies endured.
When dying held perfection,
In your eyes read the need to live.
Now you've calmly turned and walked away,
Embracing new love.
Love's betrayer.
I hear myself say 'I love you.'

Sara de Vine

The Universe

Our Universe is a mysterious place, across a great divide.
Its ever-changing facets, showing in our sky.
On a summer's day the sky is blue, with fluffy clouds anew.
A balmy breeze blowing through the trees, a time to review.
Stormy days show greyness, and an ever-changing scene.
With colours of a rainbow, shining so serene.
The sun comes out to warm the earth, with a positive effect.
A time for relaxation, and a time to reflect.

From day to night-time, stars come out and light our galaxy.
The moon casting mysterious shadows, a guide for you and me.
The night-time with its eerie silence, a sign of things at rest.
A light in the sky for travellers to help them in their quest.
Our Universe is a wonderful place, changing all the time.
A Universe so complex, across our great divide.

Kaye Sutton

LIGHT

Candle burning in the night
Giving us a tiny light
Many lights there are we love
Moon and stars to shine above
And to warm us all the day
Sun shines down with many a ray

Fire is another light
Glowing in the grate so bright
Gas and the electric light
Shining in the street at night
What a lot of lights there are
If we only look that far

Lamps of old we used to burn
And of them we sometimes yearn
Also there's electric lights
Bright and in our homes at night
Strike a match and make a light
Little night-light for a child
With a tiny light so mild.

E Gash

TOMATOES
(or a difficult poem)

In a torn, crumpled, rumpled,
brown paper bag.
On a shelf in the arctic, or
sitting on a try - which is green.
I hear the screams, I can
feel the shouts.
The pain is there, which I
never knew before,
until now.

And then the rain beats
down as the gods grab,
relentlessly, viciously, cruelly.
Survival of the fittest?
Not here, they'll all die soon.
But then the radiant rainbow
rushes in after the rain, and the
foolish feel they will be saved,
until later.

But alas, the gods have
no mercy now.
The storm starts suddenly again,
with lightning which divides
and splits everything in sight,
as easily as a tree or a shrub.
And in the salad bowl
of life they lie,
until they die.

Barbara Goddard

TIME TRAVELLER

I'm a traveller in time
I travel through the ages of man
Trying to gain knowledge and wisdom
Learning whatever I can

Yet the more I see in my travels
The more disillusioned I become
History keeps repeating itself
And the bow is replaced by the gun

Evil dictators have risen to power
With no mercy for any who oppose
Overnight a friend turns into a foe
And the doors of humanity are closed

Millions have died of hunger
When man has had plenty in store
Half the world dies of too much
And still they yearn for more

Our earth has never been abused
Like it has in this modern age
The beautiful jewel of the universe
At the mercy of man's greedy rage

The more I travel through the ages of man
The more I become ashamed of our race
Why can't we live like the animals
At least they all know their place

We're supposed to be the superior ones
Let's start proving it by our deeds
I don't want to travel through time anymore
I'm tired of seeing how mankind bleeds.

Paul Brooks

Jeffery

(A hill near Pendle)

You have been there, so you know
How the yellow cowslips grow
By The Pass
And under hedges,
Mingling on its mossy edges
With the flowers the coppice has -
How the wind blows, sweetly scented,
From the hillside clothed in heather,
And the hare in windy weather

Whirls and leaps as if demented -
How the heart-enthralling air
Calls to mind that earlier day
We were walking up that way,
Leaving thoughts of war behind.

How the bracken, golden-tinted
Made its contrast with the pines
How the yellow furze-blooms glinted
'Gainst the sombre of the grass!
And the lines of purple hills -
Antidote for all our hills.

But, best of all in beauty there -
By The Pass and under hedges -
Mingling on its mossy edges -
Were those, cowslips, wondrous fair -
You have been there, so you know!

Louis Challoner

A Handful Of Seeds

Just a handful of seeds -
But what do I see?

Bright scarlet poppies in fields bathed in sunshine,
Ripe golden corn and sweet smelling hay,
And overhead the voice of the skylark
Singing to greet each magical day.

An elegant garden, quiet and calm,
With larkspur and lupins - a sweet gentle balm
To soothe a mind or ease a pain
And bring back peace and contentment again.

A gay cottage garden, ablaze with bloom -
Blue, purple, flame - with a sweet perfume -
And love-in-a-mist as blue as the sky
And banks of white daisies like clouds floating by -
And the peaceful drone of the honey bee -
That's what a handful of seeds means to me.

Margaret Parry

SOLO

Please don't cry for me.
Please don't let those beautiful emotions
Get involved in my torment and agony.

I can't help that I'm sitting here alone,
Staring at the ceiling, watching all the emptiness,
And wondering how full it is compared to me.

Please let me do the crying.
Let me wail my dark eyes
Until these thoughts run dry.

You see, there is no light at the end of this tunnel.
All those that have loved me, have now forgotten me,
A blurred dream in their murky past.

And however hard I try to catch this supposed dream of
Happiness and fulfilment, they mock me and reject me.
After all I am but a cruel joke.

It's not all their doing though, is it?
For I always set myself up as a target
Waiting to be shot and torn to shreds.

It is my fault that I am vulnerable and sensitive,
To all the wickedness and vile that God can create.
Life is not for the feint hearted like me.

So please my loveable bundle of fun,
You can't help me through this pain.
But please remember me, for who I am.

Rather than for what I am and for whom I am not with.

Martin Woods

THE RAT'S HOME

From the depth of the stone bridge,
Looking down on the river's flow;
Not at a speed but slow, graceful, slipping over the rocks.
The rocks coated with a growth of moss,
Changing colour as the water glides over the mass of greens.
A rat, big and fat leaves the hole of its home;
Slithering into the water looking glossy as it darts forward;
Its long brown tail as straight as an arrow in flight.
In one quick movement the rat takes to the land;
Sniffs the air on sturdy hind legs,
Finding no danger it rummages round between tall grass,
Sniffing at flowers and playing with a fly.
The fun is over before it has a chance to start,
And its back to work collecting grass to make a nest.
Dry brown moss is mixed with lush grass as it goes along;
Always aware of unwelcome predators.
It's back to its run arranging the moss,
Weaving the grass to keep the young warm that's to come . . .

Alan Bowman

DID WE REALLY TRY

It takes a special kind of courage
To realise your dreams
So many things disbar you
(At least that's how it seems).

The avenues that we explore
To nowhere seem to lead
Without a clear direction
How can we succeed?

Chances come that we let pass
But make us wonder why
Can the answer truly be
That we didn't really try?

Have we maintained our place
Upon the bottom rung of life
And never knew to our disgrace
We couldn't stand the strife?

We make excuses every day
They are our stock in trade
In order to persuade ourselves
Our chance was never made.

So let us pull ourselves together
And assess our worth anew
Then get and do whatever
It is what we need to do!

R H Gunston

Men In Clogs

Where are the men in caps and dogs that
did work within the mills?
Where is the mill that drew the men for
that age and longer still?
Where is the machine that midst the drone?
the clatter and the dust?
Would draw these men, day in, day out,
to sweat for just a crust.
The mule 'set on' the spindle turned, the
cotton would twist and sway
It would 'back off' and run 'back in' and
thus another day.
They work barefoot on an oil soaked floor
the work rate so intense.
They cast their crowns and splice the
scrolls for just a few hard pence.
Line up the boxes 'doff the cops' a
fourteen hundred score.
I know those men in clogs, I walked the floor!

G Hodson

AUTUMN

Autumn came, icy tongue and all, licking the wind.
Making it bite in the morning and at night,
Still the sun petered through, a little in the day,
Before the rain came again and again,
Patter, patter it seemed to say,
One rain soaked autumn day,
Tall bedraggled foxglove spires rise and fall
against the red brick wall,
Rain splattered rose heads, spoilt and brown,
give up the ghost and hang their heads down.
Californian poppies orange and yellow close like
cocktail umbrellas,
And wait and wait for the autumn sun to warm
their faces before they've done.

J Shaw

TIME

I feel that I have known the timelessness of time
And felt her moods of restless change and tasted deep
Her sweetest gifts and drunk her potent wine.
And well I know her fickle ways when moments
Into hours she turns. Then once again the ecstasy
Of hours become as fleeting breath, and then I know
That I have trespassed down some meandering path
That leads across the threshold into eternity.

Bernard Wright

THE UNKNOWN WOMEN

They said and they laughed at you,
on that dark and still night,
they laughed at you with fear
but who was right?

They chased and caught you,
they beat you with vengeance so strong,
they left you lying there,
not knowing they were wrong.

I found you dying,
your head against the ground
I buried my head against yours,
an overcast spread around.

I picked you up and carried you,
for miles it seemed to be,
the road wearily passed me by,
as a teardrop appeared in my eye,
as I rested your limp body down.

The moon came down and the stillness,
my heartbeat oh so slow,
as I covered your sleepy body,
in the cold fresh white snow.

I left you there buried,
and slowly walked away,
my life too had ended,
that tragic wintry day.

Philip Costis

BUFFALOES

The Indian water-buffalo toils in the open fields,
Unwittingly contributing to cultivation's yields.
Its swept-back, streamlined horns suggest a beast of wondrous pace;
The rest of it is quite devoid of any sort of grace;
And though it bears its burden with an outward self-control
One suspects it bears resentment in the darkness of its soul.

The buffalo of Africa is quite a different case -
Impatient and belligerent, encountered face-to-face;
And though a host of predators include it in their diet
They view the task of catching it with obvious disquiet:
And often, as the king of beasts, the lion, limps away,
The mighty buffalo lives on, to fight another day.

Americans call wapiti 'elk', and call the real elk 'moose',
Despite the misconceptions such misnomers can produce.
But the North American bison is the misnamed beast known best -
Immortal as the 'buffalo' of the wild and woolly West;
Well, you can't trust Yanks with English, they just bend it to
their will,
And they couldn't weave a legend round a name like Bison Bill.

Derrick Coop

NOTHING ELSE

In the depths of my mind, you're by my side,
By my side smiling, no love to hide.
No love to hide, no pain to bear,
No pain to bear in this love so rare.
This love so rare, nothing more I need,
Nothing more I need; on your love I feed.
On your love I feed, there's nothing else,
Nothing else I will ever need.

Helen Hill

BRITANNIA CORNER

He sits alone on wooden bench,
His head is lowly bowed,
For what's in store tomorrow,
Can never make him proud.

The load of life, which burdens him,
Is part of life's cruel style,
You'll never see his loneliness,
Or even see him smile.

A father, son or brother,
This man could once have been,
He just sits there broken,
His thoughts of might have been.

The tide of crowds just pass him by,
As he looks on with a tear in his eye,
Another fag and a sip of wine,
The only comfort to his mind.

Although there's many there beside,
As he sits lonely watching,
Their voices mingle in the tide.
Of people passing by.

He cannot cry or ask for help,
He's done this many times,
The pain he suffers all alone,
As life keeps passing by.

Keith Rickells

THE OTHER WORLD

Can God save them?

Slowly they walk down the street,
  Their wealth in a plastic bag,
All they seek is a mug of hot tea
  To warm their cold bodies to sleep.

Can God save them?
We do not know.

Looking like ghosts, so fragile, so white,
  Clothes all tattered and torn,
Soles of their shoes almost gone,
  Feet begging for warmth.

Can God save them?
Probably so.

A growing crowd, saturated with drugs,
  Meeting the world with hectic heights,
They pushed God and man aside
  Now they are more dead than alive.

Can God save them?
He has tried in vain.

The church clock strikes the hours away,
  They part to meet again,
Finding a doorway, they settle down
  On a bed that is hard as cobbled ground.

Can God help them?
The answer is *no*.

Some sleep on through the night,
  Others moan and fight for life,
The law passes by, to help if they die.
  But God, in His mercy, forgives.

George Posnett

Ward 101

Blue uniforms, white uniforms,
Caring smiles, automated smiles,
White crisp linen, blank staring walls,
Lying in need, dying in need,
A room full of strangers,

Dripping tubes, despairing looks,
The rattle of death, the smell of decay,
Sterile in its order,
A light extinguished and efficiently tided away,

Evasive answers, pleading questions,
Floating illusions, recoveries fantasy,
Playing hopelessly, the brains merry-go-round,
Life's see-saw,
Balancing on the brink,

Changing positions, final stop,
Matron's end bed, checkout,
Harrowing anticipation, feverous lucid imagination,

No familiar face, or soothing grace,
Just clinical extended distraught in life's waning haste.

P D Taylor

SURVIVING

Think of a May morning,
Sunrise on a dew-white field,
When east light lifts a gentle mist
Like a curtain on a new play.
My footprints dark behind me
Lead back to a hole in the ground
Where we sleep now;
An earthy shelter
Damp with night smells
Which I hate.
I run with the air from fearful dreams
Of bombs with wings
Fires in the night, houses hanging
And fragmented people
That once I loved.
There is one large tree in the playing field
Of what's left of my school,
And this morning there are mushrooms
Where last night there were none,
Unexpectedly round and cool
Nudging into the day.
I sit against the scratchy bark
My chin upon my knees,
And think about my unused bed
And peaceful fragrant sleep.
Will I be here tomorrow,
More horrors in my pain-filled head,
More people gone, less to love,
A child of the endless war.
The days are long and sunny,
But the nights are even longer,
Ten of us to this shelter
A burrow beneath the school -
A safety trap of fear.

Think all the time of the morning,
Of sandbags being moved;
I push with my mind
Like a mushroom
Against being buried alive,
Until I can taste freedom
And breathe again.

Jane Ward

WISHING

(Dedicated to my younger sister - Emma)

If I had some time to spare
Without a worry, without a care
I'd look up high, look up afar
To try and find a wishing star.

Wishing I could be there with you
Wishing our visits were not so few
Wishing you were not so far away
Wishing I could see you every day.

Scunthorpe in Lincolnshire is such a long way
From the town in South Wales where you've gone to stay
Drive miles across the country to come and visit you
But every so often that's what we have to do.

Wishing you would come back home
Wishing you hadn't decided to roam
Wishing we were not so far apart
Wishing for you keeps you close in my heart.

My baby sister you'll always be
You've always meant so much to me
You moved away to start a new life
No long a baby - but somebody's wife!

Helena Devai

Remembrance

There is a vacuum in the heart of things.
Would that one had wings
Far back in time to fly.
We'll always miss those well loved faces
Last seen in dear familiar places.
Their living was not all in vain
Altho' they traversed far o'er the main.
They too held the memory dear
Of hills and vales and old ones
Bent from years of toil
Upon the soil,
Who loved it too,
But died where they had lived.
Not so, those who were not old
Who died with many in an alien land.
Some of a very noble band.
We salute you we of your generation
And hope that younger ones
Will, in times anent
Give thought to the sacrifice
Of all whose lives were spent.

B Margaret Rose

MORE ENIGMAS

Water goes down the plug hole
And always runs from left to right
Unless you're south of the equator
Then it runs the other way from sight.

But why should it be this way
Is it because the earth goes round?
Is it magnetism or something else,
Has the answer yet been found?

Why do moles live underground?
Where it's black with dark and gloom,
Why don't they come outside up top?
Where it's light and there is more room.

We know their food is down below,
But they could go down just to feed
Then come up into fresh air again
And go to eat just when there's need.

Why do some animals trust humans?
There are many others which do not.
Why can't we converse with animals
Then we really would learn a lot.

Why does water lose its salt
When it moves from sea to sky?
Does it leave the salt up there
In the clouds so very high.

Evaporation here makes the change
From saline liquid to what we drink,
This is somewhat questionable I feel,
However, that's simply what I think.

And so to end this puzzling rhyme
With such an awful lot unsaid,
It really stops me going to sleep
When I retire to my bed.

Gerard Oxley

Leading Nowhere

A long walk leading nowhere
Is what you have just took
As you wanted to think things over
Before turning one more page in the book
Of a relationship.

A long walk leading nowhere
Has took you a long time to complete
For you have managed to walk off
Some of that quarrel, some kitchen heat
That soon could have ended
A fine relationship.

A long walk leading nowhere
Has brought you home again
And after all that shouting
Tomorrow things will be the same
And you will be in the same relationship
But no one is to blame.

Keith L Powell

PASSION'S PUPPET

Woman! To you I say,
'You must leave me,
you must go,
you leeched onto
my mind and soul,
you were swamp-like passion,
destroyer of body and mind.
Now I think of you
as the Valerian's flower
beguiling by its hue
yet poison concealing.
I was an earth worm dying
in the midday sun.
Your beauty is an evil draught
your flesh a cushion of my desiring.
Even as the female
spider slowly eats her mate,
so have you punished me -
for loving you.
You are the cloven hoof,
the stiletto in my heart.'
Yet now I hear a whisper,
A disembodied voice say
'Don't go!' 'Come back!'
Could the voice be mine?
Or has passion sent me mad?

Anna Punshon

For The Dunblane Angels

The angels lined up side by side
As the gates of heaven opened wide
For the Dunblane angels, cruelly taken
with their teacher, loved, but not forsaken
And a pretty butterfly flaps its wing
As the heavenly choir starts to sing
And their message is so gentle and sweet
for they know, one day, united you'll meet
Look for me in the stars at night
for I'll be there to bring love and light
look for me in the skies so blue
and know that I'm looking down on you.
Dry your tears and don't be sad
for no-one can take the years we had
We'll be with our loved ones every day
and sharing our love every step of the way
One day we will meet again
And then there will be no more pain.

Corinne Tuck

All That Matters To Me

Together with you, is how I want to be.
You're all that matters, that matters to me.
Your sparkling smile, brightens my every day.
In your warm loving arms, that's where I'll stay.
Looking deep into your eyes, so blue like the sea.
You're all that matters, that matters to me.
I've already many memories, wonderful memories of you
I hope for many more, now we are a two.
I feel I'm walking on air, it's how I want to be.
You're all that matters, that matters to me.
Whenever I need you, you are there.
To hug me, talk to me, show me you care.
I'm in a dream, that's how I want to be.
You're all that matters, that matters to me.
You make me happy, when we are together.
I want to stay in your arms, in your arms forever.

Jodie Booth (16)

Tea For Two

A clink of cups, a tinkling of laughter.
'Well, I thought you should hear. It's not what you fear.'
Surfeit of sweets. Confection of cakes.
'Well I never!' 'We must get together.'
Sorte of sibilants. Heaps of aspirates.
Then suddenly their eyes met . . .
Silence!
The earth stopped, then tilted on its axis.
His manhood quickened, her nipples tightened.
All sound stopped. Everyone else faded away.
Just the two alone, a million, billion miles away
From the stirring spoons, and nickel knives.
Sardine sandwiches. Wittering wives.
His mouth shaped one word, and across the room,
Her eyes observed and sent back the reply.
From two ends of the room they converged on the door
And escaped together into the dusk.
Away from all the gossip, all the gobbling
Away they fled to their own dream world.
Unaware as they sped down the street
That they would be part of the next conversation piece
That they had provided the next tea-time treat.

Polly Bennison

SLIPSTREAM

Life is a river flowing along
Starting as just a small stream
Each rise in the tide supporting the strong
Each fall destroying a dream

Some folks slip by unheeded
Life over before it's begun
Some neither loved or needed
Some whose praises are sung.

We are only a drop in the ocean
It pauses for never a one
Continues its tide and motion
Forever journeying on.

Joan Walker

TENNYSON COUNTRY

In Tennyson country, where pure is the air,
There's time to stand and time to stare.
No busy traffic with its fumes and noise,
And the mind can dwell on nature's joys,
Of Tennyson's brook and the peaceful scene,
Where the sky of blue meets the Lincolnshire green.

His brook still flows by on its merry way
Past farmyards and bridges and sunbeams at play.
And peace descends as you stand and stare
Far from city life with its bustle and care,
And the water flows by so pure and so clean
Reflecting the blue o'er the Lincolnshire green.

Should the poet return, where once he did roam,
He'd still approve of his childhood home.
For little has changed from days gone by,
The trees reach up to greet the sky
And the birds and the bees here reign supreme,
Where the sky of blue meets the Lincolnshire green.

Pat Gooding

UNTITLED

Don't hesitate to say 'I love you'
To all you hold most dear,
You could regret not doing so,
When year, after rushing year - you get older.

Don't bear ill-will or hold grudges,
Give a hand and show you care,
A moment in time is all that it takes,
Other's happiness means you are there - with love.

You'll feel greater comfort inside you,
You'll feel calm, and steady and strong,
If you show the one you hold most dear,
That with love, life just rolls along.

Vera Homer

Trinity

We have three powers:
Thought, feeling and will.
Thought fills the hours
And is rarely still.
Feeling is evident
When we are moved,
Most commonly consequent
When we are loved.
Will is a 'will-o-the-wisp',
Strong now, weak then.
'I am determined,' we lisp,
And then 'give in' again.
These three in balance
Give us stability
So let each one advance
To gain compatibility.

David W Hill

Mother Tongue

Like my palm -
the grooves and dips of it,
I know my mother's voice

Or a psalm at the age of ten,
the deliverance then
of lines in time.

It's a tracing of maps,
these accents and flaps
of tongue.

Is this then where I belong -
after all foreign emancipation
and education?

But, I could hear her still
through water or sleep
and be home.

Lorraine Fothergill

Hidden Beauty

The warmth of sun against my skin
That tells me that it's fine,
The damp sweet smell of new mown grass
Is easy to define.

The velvet feel of blossomed rose
Whose perfume fills the air,
The lavender that draws the bees,
The buzz that warns they're there.

The spicy herbs we grow to eat
Too numerous to mention,
Bring scents delicious, musty sweet,
Deserving my attention.

The sighted see the colours
But can miss the touch and sound,
That echoes if you listen
In God's garden all around.

Irene Carter

Peace And Quiet

Each day I try to do my best
I feel so low, I need a rest
I always start with so much zest
But in the end I have to rest.

I love my family very much
It takes all my time keeping up
Work, cooking, shopping and more
Then someone's knocking on the door.

The telephone rings and I implore
Please, please, Oh! No more.
A neighbour calls for help with her car
And I go out and give it a jar.

These days are really hard I find
I always seem to be behind
I feel so low I need a rest
Oh! To be my old self again, full of zest.

M Coleby

ANGLIAN SUMMER

A village, the church tower
stained glass, hazy shower
A bell tolls through the mist
sullen time-on-metal kiss.

Apples smother orchard trees
resting heavy 'neath the leaves
Sorry scarecrow, man of straw
wiley rooks and ravens caw.

A reddened sun alights the plain
courting twilight once again
And the twig-fire gently wanes
pluming shrouds for faded flames.

E M Wakely

Panic Attack

In the depths of despair, swirls of blackness all around,
enclosing me, smothering me, choking me.

Panic rises up, I want to lash out, scream, shout, run,
but this is no evil enemy lurking outside in the shadows,
it can't be seen, can't be touched, it doesn't speak.

There is nowhere to run, nowhere to hide, there is no escape,
for the enemy is *Me.*

Sue Desney Hudson

UNTITLED

I have many happy memories,
tender moments shared.
the wonder of our new-born child,
your arms around me when I wept,
you laughed with me when I was happy
and shared my tears when I was sad.
We were two halves that made a whole,
and I love you still; and I miss you still.

Why did you die? I do not know,
I only know the pain I feel.
I am not whole; I am alone.
I need your arms to hold me close,
your laughter and your tears.
I wanted to grow old with you
to share with you our life
But you were taken from me and many
years have passed.
Our children now have grown and gone
and that's as it should be.
I wait, my love, impatiently until God
calls for me.

Shirley Ledwith

The Tiger

Neither sea nor land
ere the Dutchman cut his drain
arrow straight, ribbon on black earth
mercurial reflection
of a silver leaded sky
The sleeping churches
of island towns soaring above
weeping meres and pointed reeds,
landmarks for life
against an infinite sky.
While the cry of waterfowl,
more than any human can
echoes the fear and loneliness
of wind lost birds
and of mortal Fenland man.

And from the house of Fenland brick
and slated roof
which stand above the drain
candlelight spills yellow
from the public bar
through open frosted window panes.
And in it, by a fragile fire
Old Jeb sips his Elgoods ale
wiping his lips with grimy hand
rheumy eyes in the dancing flames,
his mind on times of happiness,
the time of his youth with a Fenland lass.

A bell calls time, he makes to rise
and shuffles towards the door.
He walks out into the night
and along the bank, Forty Foot,
against the dark and windy sky.
And he walks as he has for
all his years and days,
eyes cast down,
lest a meeting chanced
with Black Shuck's dread and fatal gaze.

Brian Clark

THE DOOR

Not at death's door,
Yet in the corridor of life that leads to it.
Plenty of rest and I can't even see it.
Try to be busy and I can almost reach up
and turn the handle.
And let in the wonderful light that lives
beyond the door.

I've done too much, I'm like a helium balloon,
Kept on earth only by a thin string.
Wanting to soar upwards to heaven, towards the light.
Sit down, rest, it's not yet time
to cut the string.

Tied to earth by bonds of love,
Feel the pain, know I'm fading,
Want to soar high above,
God's work for me, unfinished, here below,
Perhaps another day I'll go.

They ask so much, they don't understand,
How hard it is for me to stay,
How flimsy the cord that keeps me here,
One small slip and I'm up and away.

Pauline Merill

PASSIVE PRINCESS

Your gentle frost freezes
As you withdraw into
Your dungeon of silence.

Coolly gazing through
The bars you forged
With hot, angry fear.

Impenetrable,
the light narrowed down
To prison spars

Never reaching the corners
Of your entombed soul
Passive princess

Locked in a dark world
Of your own making
Where gratitude

Makes a feast
From a crumb of comfort
Thrown by some other

Tormented soul.

Lee Thomas

A Moon Has Risen Through A Broken Mountain

I'm sitting here on the chair again, and
I have found
the voice
again,

the voice that's like a pair of eyes.

A moon has risen through a broken mountain.

It's so often
that one can have the voice,
that sometimes
it will always be
there

and then the pen fails, the page is dull

and somewhere a light can fail.

The release is not there.
I swell, but
threaten not to burst
into air,

holding myself in the gesture of despair.

I'm sitting here on the chair again, for
I have found
the voice
again,

the voice that's like a pair of eyes

beautiful and broken each time.

Geof Wood

BEHIND BLUE EYES

If you could look behind blue eyes,
What do you think you'd see?
Not some arrogant perception,
Of how you'd like it to be

No what you'd see would be quite real,
It would make your blind heart see,
No matter how you'd have it different,
What is behind those blue eyes is me.

The sights that only they perceive,
Can mask truths, to see what they believe,
They can impair anything immorally
To fit into a world that only they can see.

Who sees exactly what these blue eyes see,
Who sees all the hills to climb, none but me,
Who knows what goes on in there I think not you,
Or your harsh condemnations couldn't ring true.

They can transfix on beauty and hope when there's none,
And give strength to the weaknesses harboured by some,
they can also express fear, delight and surprise,
But none but me can see behind these blue eyes.

Though the heart and brain may assert control,
the eyes are the windows to everyone's soul,
You can run from life, but you cannot hide.
For the eyes tell all secrets secreted inside.

A pair of eyes that shed no tears,
The eyes that cloud over in premature years,
Are filled with untrue uncouth dishonesty,
And are far too sad for me to want to see.

Even a pair of long legs with well structured thighs,
I'd ignore just to see behind honest blue eyes . . .

R T Richardson

NIGHT TRAVELLER

In the silence of the night,
Whilst others sleep, my thoughts take flight.
Down through the years they gently glide
Into my childhood countryside.
Deep in the shade of old woodland
Where sentinels of bracken stand,
Beyond the fronds so proud and green
A blur of blue transforms the scene.
For violets raise their pretty heads
To decorate soft mossy beds,
Reaching down to touch the sedge
Nestling at cool water's edge.
Sweetly the beck still ripples by,
Washing its pebbles with gentle sigh.
This shallow brook, my Pipes of Pan,
From bank to bank, a child's span.
Then over the stream, up the Ride
For this is where the glow-worms hide,
Where butterfly and dragonfly
Caress the air from earth to sky.
My beck has now grown wide and deep.
I hear the splash as fishes leap.
And somewhere in the trees so tall
A pheasant shrieks his warning call.
Rhododendrons form a screen
To shield The Lodge, a pretty scene.
Windows gleam with diamond panes,
Ivy twisting around the frames.
Each side a little iron gate
A hedge of box, so neat and straight.
Crunch of gravel, softness of grass,
Sweet scent of lilies as I pass.

When moonbeams cast a mellow glow,
When foxes from their lairs go,
When owls swoop down, so silently,
My thoughts wing back, to reality.
There is no wood, my friends all say,
The Lodge has gone . . . 'twas in the way
Of a fine motel and new highway.
But I'll return to childhood sights
In the silence of my nights!

Joy M Lacy

The End's Beginning

When the earth is sleeping
And the dawn is nigh,
The shepherd, He will come a calling,
On the wings of the wind will fly.

Trumpets will proclaim His coming
And lightning fill the sky,
As strong men stand and tremble
Alas in vain will cry.

Multitudes will stand
Transfixed on every shore,
And gaze in wonder upon the face
That's not a fable anymore.

Hear the distant drumming
Descending from the sky,
March on ye patient sleepers
As centuries are swept aside.

For they have all been watching
And waiting for the call,
Already left behind, hindrent, aching bodies,
Just shells laid, side by side.

No one will be forgotten,
No one can step aside.
No one can shun from judgement,
For the Lord had prophisied.

William Arthur Thomas

The Old Apple Tree

A new day begins as I slip from my bed,
the night sky has changed to deep rosy red.
The birds fill the air with their shrill morning song
The dark lonely night has once again gone.

A breeze stirs the leaves of the old apple tree,
I smile to myself as I remember how we
on a bright summer day so long long ago.
Planted the twiglet and hoped it would grow.

How happy we were in our first little home,
The smell of fresh paint and the lawn neatly mown
The roses especially were your pride and joy,
Then later that year with the first fall of snow,
The love in your eyes as you held our first boy.

How little we knew what that next year would bring,
As the cuckoo's first song did herald the spring.
For this was the year that near broke my heart,
When war was declared and tore us apart.

Our second son was born as you fought far away,
and each night I held him I'd kneel down and pray.
that the Lord would watch over you and keep you from harm
Until I'd hold you once more again safe in my arms.

We met just once more on a brief summer leave
When the young apple tree was full of green leaves
We filled all our days with memories to store,
for the long lonely nights that would part us once more.

A swing dangles now from that old apple tree
Your grandsons play there and I wish you could see.
How happy and strong they're both going to be
As they play in the branches of that poor old tree.

Marjorie Fovargue

INFORMATION

We hope you have enjoyed reading this book - and that you will continue to enjoy it in the coming years.

If you like reading and writing poetry drop us a line, or give us a call, and we'll send you a free information pack.

Write to :-

Poetry Now Information
1-2 Wainman Road
Woodston
Peterborough
PE2 7BU
(01733) 230746